JAGUAR

Graham Robson

SHIRE PUBLICATIONS

Published in Great Britain in 2012 by Shire Publications Ltd, Midland House, West Way, Botley, Oxford OX2 0PH, United Kingdom.

44-02 23rd Street, Suite 219, Long Island City, NY 11101, USA.

E-mail: shire@shirebooks.co.uk   www.shirebooks.co.uk

© 2012 Graham Robson.

A CIP catalogue record for this book is available from the British Library.

Shire Library no. 709.   ISBN-13: 978 0 74781 203 6

Graham Robson has asserted his right under the Copyright, Designs and Patents Act, 1988, to be identified as the author of this book.

Designed by Tony Truscott Designs, Sussex, UK and typeset in Perpetua and Gill Sans.

Printed in China through Worldprint Ltd.

12 13 14 15 16   10 9 8 7 6 5 4 3 2 1

COVER IMAGE
The third-generation XK model was the XK150, which was introduced in 1957, complete with a much modified style, and with four-wheel disc brakes. It was the first series-production Jaguar to use them.

TITLE PAGE IMAGE
The XK120 sports car was previewed in 1948 and soon proved that it could exceed 125 mph, making it the world's fastest production car at this time.

CONTENTS PAGE IMAGE
This was the badge that graced Jaguar cars from their introduction in 1945. It would be modified in later years.

ACKNOWLEDGEMENTS
I would like to thank all my contacts, colleagues, and friends at Jaguar, both in the UK and in the USA, for allowing me to use the factory-sourced illustrations. Their pictorial archive, along with the facts and figures which are also available to serious researchers, make it a joy to work with the company.

Shire Publications is supporting the Woodland Trust, the UK's leading woodland conservation charity, by funding the dedication of trees.

CONTENTS

IN THE BEGINNING: SIDECARS AND REBODIED SPECIALS

THE DIFFERENCE BETWEEN the Jaguar car's original ancestors – motorcycle sidecars built in Blackpool – and today's luxury automobiles, is total. The story of Jaguar is a fascinating one that combines elegant styling, ambition, high performance and commercial good sense.

Although the name 'Jaguar' was not applied to a car until 1935, the machinery that inspired it first took shape in 1922. William Lyons, born and raised in Blackpool, started work for Crossley Motors in Manchester in 1918 and then dabbled with various short-term jobs in Blackpool, before meeting William Walmsley. The two young men soon got together, in 1922, to start producing motorcycle sidecars in tiny numbers, and before long it fell to Lyons to bring artistic flair to the shaping of new products. Building up to ten sidecars every week, the new concern was called the Swallow Sidecar Company – which is why the first cars that they were soon to start producing were known as 'SS' machines.

Over the next few years the business blossomed. First SS produced simple bodies, for fixing to other companies' chassis; then they began to make their own chassis, and still the demand grew. By 1926 Lyons (who always seemed to have more entrepreneurial ambition than Walmsley) was looking to go beyond sidecars: they began to deal in coachbuilding, repainting, retrimming or otherwise modifying other companies' cars, and they soon set about designing complete car bodies of their own.

The first SS-bodied car – an Austin Seven – followed in 1927, having altogether sleeker lines than the machines being produced by Austin itself at Longbridge. First seen by the public in the specialist motoring press, in May 1927, the cute little aluminium-bodied Austin Seven was available as an open-top two-seater for £175, or as a closed coupé for £185. *The Autocar* suggested that 'The latest, and certainly one of the most attractive-looking bodies arranged for this car, is the Swallow saloon-coupé, built by the Swallow Sidecar and Coachbuilding Co...'

Business was brisk from the start, but Swallow had an immediate problem in that their cramped little works at Blackpool could not produce

Opposite: William Lyons began his business career in Blackpool, styling and constructing sidecars for motorcycles.

Sir William Lyons, 1901–86, the founder of Jaguar.

more than two cars a day, the varnishing shop being the limiting factor. By comparison, the company was already building up to one hundred sidecar bodies every week.

Lyons did not allow this to hold the company back, for he was thinking far into the future. Only months after the Austin Seven Swallow had been shown, the company produced its second offering, which was significantly larger (and therefore more costly): the Morris-Cowley Swallow, which sold for £210. The problem of space, however, soon came to a head when Lyons was introduced to Henlys Ltd, the big London-based motor traders, for they placed an immediate order for five hundred cars, and demanded delivery at the rate of twenty cars every week. Furthermore, they wanted to see a saloon version of the original style produced as well, which meant more work for Lyons, who was now becoming the styling genius he would remain for more than forty years.

This was the style of the original Swallow sidecars for which William Lyons was responsible.

Soon the Blackpool premises were bursting at the seams, and the tight-knit little workforce was working huge amounts of overtime to keep up with demand. Lyons and Walmsley then concluded that they would have to move

away from Blackpool. The centre of Britain's motor industry at that time was unquestionably Coventry, and Lyons spent much time there searching for new premises. A suitable site was eventually found in the shape of a disused shell-filling factory in Whitmore Park, Foleshill, Coventry.

When the factory was ready in 1928, the company invited all its Blackpool staff to move south (which most of them did), took on more workers in Coventry itself, and was up and running only days after the complex move of cars, part-built cars, components and equipment had been accomplished. No sooner had this been done than the company started improving the property it had leased; they resurfaced the access road and secured the right to expand into other empty buildings alongside. Their target of producing fifty cars every week was rapidly reached.

Before long, Lyons began to look around for new products to add to the Austin Seven cars, which were still the company's staple product. Several new models were introduced, some selling better than others, the theory being that Swallow would produce completely new body styles, but that the

Series production of Swallow sidecars at Blackpool in the mid-1920s.

The Austin Swallow saloon of 1927 was the first complete car to be styled by William Lyons. His styling career would cover forty-five years.

original rolling chassis would be retained. Among these models were an Alvis-Swallow, a Fiat 509-Swallow and a Swift-Swallow, but all these were soon to become financially insignificant in comparison with Swallow's next big tie-up – which was with Standard.

The timing was important. Standard, then and later an important car manufacturer in Coventry, had been in decline, but was rapidly being revived by a new general manager, Captain John Black, who wanted to expand the company's sales. The opportunity came almost at once, when Lyons worked his styling magic on the latest Standard Nine. By early 1930 a new Standard Nine-Swallow was on sale, for a mere £250, and was soon joined by another Standard-based car, this running on the much larger six-cylinder Ensign chassis.

This was only the beginning of what would develop into a close, tempestuous, but ultimately climactic relationship. William Lyons wanted to push ahead with his ideas for future cars and saw Standard (for whom John Black was similarly ambitious) as a suitable business associate. *The Autocar* of 31 July 1931 summarised what happened next:

> 'SS' is the symbol adopted for a new car which will be put on the market in
> due course… The mechanism of the car has been developed from the 1932
> type Standard Sixteen chassis…

The first step towards the birth of Jaguar was under way.

Left: How car shapes changed in sixty years: the Austin Swallow two-seater is closer to the camera, with the 'XJ40' type of XJ6 saloon in the background.

Below: Once established, Austin Swallows sold well, so the small factory at Blackpool was soon overcrowded.

SS, SS-JAGUAR AND THE SS100

WHEN THE London Motor Show opened at Olympia in October 1931, the very first 'SS' car went on display. Like all such models that were to follow, the SS1, as it was known, was sleek, wickedly attractive, and offered at what looked like a very low price. At £310, it seemed to offer virtues that few longer-established rivals could match. These were attributes that all future SS, SS-Jaguar and Jaguar cars would share. Considering that the British economy was then in the depths of the Depression, and United Kingdom car sales were still in decline, this looked – and was – astonishingly brave.

Swallow's progress, however, had been remarkable. First, it had built motorcycle bodies; then it had built car bodies; next it had developed its own visual character; and now here was the first of what would be a family of entirely specialised machines. This, for a company that was still under-capitalised, and which owned very little heavy machinery, was an amazing achievement.

Although Standard was to supply and assemble complete chassis, engines and all the running gear, that chassis was special and not to be shared with anyone else, and Swallow would produce its own bodywork. Two basic cars were available at first: the SS1, with a side-valve six-cylinder Standard engine; and a smaller SS2, complete with small Standard four-cylinder power unit. As the seasons passed, more and more different body styles – coupés, convertibles and eventually saloons – would all be put on sale.

It was typical of William Lyons that he started cautiously and pragmatically, for, although the cars looked stunning, they remained mechanically simple. Side-valve engines – even the original 2,663cc-engined 20-hp SS1 – were not very powerful, so for that car a top speed of only about 70 mph was available, but customers forgave them this in their eagerness to own such wickedly and sinuously shaped machines.

Surprisingly, the larger-engined SS1s outsold the SS2s by a considerable margin, so that in four years 4,254 SS1s were sold, compared with 1,796 SS2s. By 1935, with the British economy recovering rapidly, nearly two thousand cars were being built every year.

Opposite:
The first 'Jaguar'-badged car, the 2½-litre SS-Jaguar of 1935, posed outside the door of the SS Cars company in Coventry.

This was the first ever SS car, as revealed at the Olympia Motor Show in the autumn of 1931.

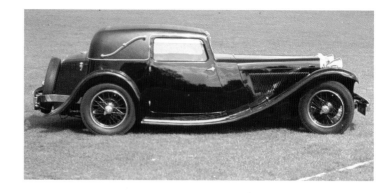

But Lyons was not yet satisfied. From late 1933, a new company called SS Cars was set up, to take over from Swallow. By the beginning of 1935 that company was ready to attract more working capital by floating itself on the Stock Exchange, and at this point William Walmsley sold his share of the business and left the company he had helped to found. For the next four decades – until he retired from active business in 1972 – William Lyons therefore became the single most important, powerful and decisive manager in the company.

By 1935 the SS1 range included this very smart four-seater Tourer.

In 1935 SS began to design a new range of cars – not only with their own special chassis, but with overhead-valve engines, and radically new

styling as well. Although Standard would still supply engines and running gear, the entire motor car was now to be assembled at Foleshill, starting from the bare chassis frame. With the help of engine specialist Harry Weslake, the rugged side-valve Standard 'Six' was converted to a more powerful overhead-valve operation, and the 'Four' would follow suit two years later.

For the first time, therefore, SS needed a chief engineer to control all this enterprise; this was when William Heynes joined the company, soon

During the mid-1930s there was a short-lived vogue for what were called 'streamlined' body styles – this being the SS 'Airline' of 1935.

13

Bill Heynes joined Jaguar as chief engineer in 1935 and directed the engineering of all Jaguars, including the race cars, until the end of the 1960s.

becoming Lyons's most trusted associate. They would stay together for the next thirty years. In the meantime, a brand-new body style was developed and, to celebrate its arrival, Lyons cast around for a new name. After considering the names of many other wild animals, he settled on 'Jaguar'. At a stroke, the 'SS' brand, which was just four years old, became 'SS-Jaguar', and the company took another step towards worldwide fame.

Production, sales and the new company's reputation all soared in the late 1930s, especially after an even more powerful 125-bhp/3.5-litre engine was developed, an all-steel bodyshell was designed, and a two-seater called the SS100 went on sale.

The SS100 was what would now be called a 'flagship' model, a true two-seater sports car, with performance approached by very few rivals at the time. Sold with 2.5- or 3.5-litre versions of the six-cylinder engine, it could reach up to 100 mph and had styling that made almost every other British car

The SS100, a rakish two-seater, was capable of 100 mph when fitted with the optional 3½-litre engine. In the background is an XK8.

of the period look dowdy. Even so, the price of the most powerful version was a mere £445 (there was no VAT, sales tax or purchase tax in those halcyon days), and SS-Jaguar began to overtake other Coventry-based car-makers (such as Riley and Triumph) for the first time.

By 1939 SS-Jaguar was making more than five thousand cars every year, the existing factory at Foleshill was full, and the company was looking for ways to expand and to make even more. This was remarkable – a real success story for a company that was still controlled, both functionally and financially, by one man, William Lyons. From building just 776 SS cars in its first full year (1931–2), within eight years it had taken over other buildings alongside the originals and had expanded production sevenfold, all without having to manufacture anything other than its own bodyshells.

SS-Jaguar, however, had great ambitions, and, if the Second World War had not broken out in 1939, these would surely have been achieved in short order. Not only did the company want to adopt independent front suspension for its elegant machines (this was still seen as something of a novelty in Britain's motor industry), but it wanted to begin more systemised assembly by buying up a body-building concern (Motor Panels), and to start manufacturing its own six-cylinder engines.

But, in September 1939, Adolf Hitler's military forces invaded Poland, so Britain and France declared war on Germany to defend Poland's right to peace, and the world changed – for ever.

The shape and character of all Jaguars, of whatever period, were always characteristic of the type of car William Lyons wanted to sell. Here we see an XK120 (1940s), an SS100 (1930s), and an E-Type (1960s) posed together. Behind them is drop-head XK8.

POST-WAR EXPANSION:
THE XK-ENGINED ERA

IT TOOK TIME FOR SS-Jaguar's war effort to swing into action, but after six years a creditable output had been achieved. A new building in Foleshill, originally intended to produce Manchester bombers, and which dwarfed the original factory that SS had occupied since 1928, went on to build Wellington, Whitley, Stirling, Mosquito and Meteor aircraft frames and wings, along with thousands of components for other aircraft, and aero engines.

The buildings were bombed only once, in 1941, and even this damage was speedily repaired, so activity was continuous, and the variety of jobs tackled was enormous. Once the final pre-war build of new cars had been completed in 1939–40, there was no time to build new private cars, but a wide variety of sidecars, trailers and similar automotive add-ons kept the existing car-building expertise ticking over.

That was not all. On the rare occasions that they had any spare time, managers and engineers would sit down to consider the company's future. Central to this was the decision taken, before the war ended, to drop the initials 'SS' from the company name (those letters had acquired sinister connotations from their use by the Schutzstaffel, the ruthless German paramilitary defence corps), so the name 'Jaguar', on its own, at last came to prominence.

Three other vital decisions were also made to underpin the company's future: Jaguar would not develop its links with Motor Panels (that business would be sold); it would take over the six-cylinder engine-manufacturing equipment from Standard (which would nevertheless continue to supply four-cylinder units); and in the long term it would develop its own brand-new family of engines. This was the period when the famous XK engine was conceived, and when the power units that would power the company's famous cars for the next forty years came into being. Although there was no time for prototypes to be built, or for cars to be tested at first, time was found to plan, to scheme, to discuss, and to make ready for the peace that would surely come.

Opposite:
The XK120 assembly line at Foleshill in 1950 – already full, and very busy. The entire operation would be moved to Browns Lane in 1952.

During the Second World War Jaguar's workforce produced many major components for the Whitley bomber.

At the height of the war, managers were obliged to carry out fire-watching duties at the Foleshill factory, in case of incendiary attack from enemy aircraft. Lyons made sure that a close-knit little group of people – himself, Bill Heynes, engine designer Claude Baily and development engineer Walter Hassan among them – were always rostered to work together on Sunday nights, when they found time to discuss all manner of engineering schemes for post-war models.

Because William Lyons had not latterly enjoyed working in harness with Standard (and particularly with Sir John Black), chief among these plans was

Bill Heynes, Walter Hassan, Harry Mundy and Claude Baily were all part of an illustrious Jaguar engine-design team in post-war years.

the intention to design new engines. After much development work had been carried out, initially on paper, and eventually on the test beds, a closely related range of new four-cylinder and six-cylinder engines, all with twin-overhead-camshaft cylinder heads, spanning 2.0 litres ('Four') to 3.4 litres ('Six'), was developed, and thus the XK range began its long and illustrious career. Although the 'Four' was launched in 1948, and occasionally seen in public thereafter, it was never put on sale, while the 'Six' became Jaguar's general-purpose power unit, which could be put to a whole range of uses.

This, however, is to jump ahead a little. Immediately after the war ended in 1945, Jaguar (now without the 'SS') converted its factories back to civilian use, completed the installation of machinery to build the ex-Standard engines, and started to build private cars again. The elegant 1.5-litre, 2.5-litre and 3.5-litre saloons that had been produced in 1938 and 1939 were revived; drop-head coupé derivatives soon followed, and by 1948 production was again up to more than four thousand cars a year.

Then came the first true innovations. Although Lyons had originally wanted to introduce new chassis, engines and styles together, he was frustrated by post-war shortages and the need to join a queue for new-type bodies at his bodyshell suppliers, Pressed Steel. He also came to realise that it might be financially difficult to achieve everything at once.

In 1948, therefore, he pragmatically elected to introduce a brand-new chassis, complete with torsion-bar independent front suspension, and to phase in a new style of saloon (the Mark V) to sit on top of it, but to hold back the XK engine for the future. That was the original plan, but even before the

Launched in 1948, the Mark V featured a completely new chassis, with independent front suspension and this graceful five-seater body style, but still used the late-1930s type of overhead-valve engine.

19

Jaguar also produced some Mark V drop-head coupés – this car being photographed, much later, alongside a 1998 XJR.

Earl's Court Motor Show of that year (the first London show to be held after the war) he also decided to rush through the development of a graceful new two-seater sports car, the XK120, which would become the first to use the twin-cam XK engine.

The XK120 was an immediate success in overseas markets; this batch was destined for sale in North America.

The appearance, and the potential, of the XK120, caused a sensation. Whereas the Mark V was something of a throwback to pre-war shapes and equipment, the XK120 was the sort of car that caused every red-blooded

driver, whether British or foreign, to go weak at the knees. It was not merely that it looked sleek, and that it could exceed 120 mph (which made it a true supercar by post-war standards), but that it was to be sold at the astonishingly cheap price, in the United Kingdom, of £1,263.

Before long, not only had the XK120 proved every claim made for it, by winning production car races outright, and by achieving an authenticated 132 mph in a straight-line demonstration in Belgium, but it greatly exceeded every original estimate of sales. Jaguar had cautiously thought they might sell two hundred such cars, but they soon had to have the bodyshell retooled for bigger quantities, and more than twelve thousand were delivered in six years.

The next outstandingly pleasant shock came when the Mark VII saloon appeared in 1950. This was a car that combined the chassis of the Mark V with the XK engine, all hidden by a larger, but graceful-looking, six-seater saloon shell. It sold at an attractive price and could easily exceed 100 mph.

Now that the last trace of pre-war engineering had been cast aside – styles, engines and titles were all modern – Jaguar could export their cars

The Mark VII, which went on sale in 1950/1, was the first Jaguar saloon to use the famous XK engine. Although it was a large car (here it is compared with the XK120), it could exceed 100 mph with ease.

with relish, particularly to the United States, where the 'Jagwah' (as it was pronounced there) was seen as simultaneously trendy and traditional. Starting from scratch in 1947, when just seven cars were sent to North America, Jaguar exported 1,050 there in 1949–50, and 3,339 in 1951–2. As more than six thousand cars a year were being produced for all markets, the factory at Foleshill simply could not accommodate any more, even though the original 40,000 square feet occupied in 1928 had expanded to 600,000 square feet.

The search began for alternative or additional premises, especially when an application to the government to expand the Foleshill factory was turned down on planning grounds. However, this was not to be a repeat of the 1928 upheaval, when Swallow had been obliged to uproot itself from Blackpool and set down new roots in Coventry, more than 100 miles away. This time there was spare capacity in the city (mostly buildings used for war work that had rapidly been emptied after 1945), and Jaguar chose a former Daimler company factory in Browns Lane, Allesley, just 2 miles from Foleshill in another suburb of Coventry. The move, initiated in 1951, was eventually completed late in 1952, which gave the company more than a million square feet in which to work (which was swiftly filled). The older Foleshill plant was sold off (to Dunlop).

The Mark VII was the first Jaguar 100-mph saloon, but there would be many more to follow in future years.

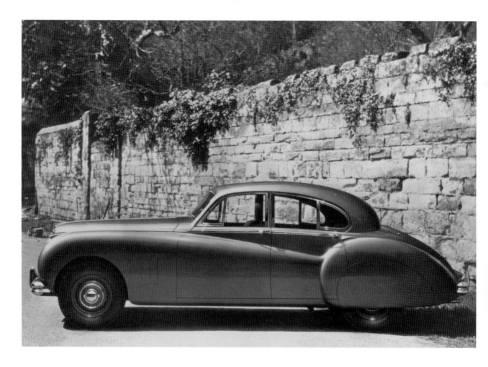

Accordingly, at a time when Jaguar was already running flat out, with waiting lists building up all round the world, the big move took place. Somehow there were no major hiccups, and annual production immediately rose to more than ten thousand cars in 1952–3, and the company's glamorous reputation continued to grow. This, the start of Britain's new 'Elizabethan age', was a stimulating time to be in business, and Jaguar took every advantage of it.

Not only were the company's two staple model ranges – the XK120 sports cars and the Mark VII saloons – extremely popular, but Jaguar had also begun winning world-class races, while other technical innovations continued to flow. Jaguar in racing is covered in another chapter, but the reason why the company's road cars were so very successful must be emphasised here.

Continuity was the key factor, for Jaguar made certain that the same sure hand (and eye) – that of company founder William Lyons himself – would shape the new models for many years, and that the same engineering team, led by Bill Heynes, would oversee all the technical innovations. For these reasons, anyone with a sensitive eye for a line or a trend could easily relate the evolution of the XK family from one type to another – XK120 in 1948, XK140 in 1954, and XK150 in 1957 – and see where and how the racing C-Types and D-Types fitted in too.

In the meantime, the already famous XK engine was soon joined by super-powerful versions (the 3.4-litre engine was rated at 250 bhp when the D-Type racing sports car was revealed in 1954), and overdrive transmission, then automatic transmission, became increasingly popular optional extras, while all manner of work carried on behind the scenes. Disc-brake development was to be seen in one corner, independent rear suspension in another, and even an exotic 9-litre V8 engine project for a possible Ministry of Defence contract in yet another.

The most important advance, however, came in 1955, when the company introduced its very first unit-construction saloon car – the 2.4-litre model. After many years of producing strictly traditional-type Jaguars, all built around a separate chassis frame, it was time to move on. The existing cars had gradually grown slightly too large and too heavy, and the clientele was now clamouring for a smaller Jaguar again.

It was typical of Lyons that for this major investment he took advice where it was needed, but stayed loyal to his own company resources where possible. To make this new car, he would adapt Browns Lane to allow more cars to be built, he would style the compact four-door car himself, he would authorise the development of a smaller version of the XK engine (2.4 litres instead of 3.4 litres), but he would then rely totally on Pressed Steel of Oxford to engineer and manufacture the unit-construction (chassis-less) bodyshells to make it all possible.

Even though Jaguar was building four to five hundred cars every week by the late 1950s, the craftsmen were still able to spend time on traditional methods of trimming the sports cars.

Jaguar announced its first 'small' unit-construction car in 1955, this being the 112-bhp 2.4-litre 2.4 model. When the larger-engined 3.4 was added to this range, it became Jaguar's best-seller of the period.

It was a huge gamble, but it succeeded. The new 2.4 went on sale in 1955, with a relatively unstressed 112-bhp/2.4-litre engine, but at a remarkably low price of just £1,299. Sales, and accordingly, production leapt ahead, passing twelve thousand a year in 1956 and looking set to rise in the future.

William Lyons had now been knighted – henceforth he was always officially and affectionately known as 'Sir William'; an extremely fast derivative of the 2.4 – the 210-bhp 3.4-litre saloon model, which used a full-size XK engine – was almost ready for launch, and the

third-generation XK sports car, the XK150, was also about to reach the showrooms; everything looked good for the burgeoning Coventry car-maker.

But early in the evening of 12 February 1957, when all but a few staff had gone home, fire broke out at one end of the main assembly halls, rapidly consuming up to a third of the factory itself, wrecking the northern end of the assembly lines, destroying scores of newly built cars, and badly damaging many others. Luckily, no one was seriously hurt in this conflagration, but the business was badly hit.

Amazingly, rudimentary new assembly lines were opened up within days. Production forged ahead – it would reach 17,552 in 1957–8 – and the new models were launched as planned. It was typical of Jaguar's determined spirit that within a year not only was the Browns Lane site back to normal, but the entire Jaguar operation was now developing as never before. It was almost as if the fire had acted as a barrier between the 'old' company and the 'new'. In the next few years, not only would more and more cars be made, but sensational new models would be launched, Jaguar would absorb other famous companies, and it would eventually become part of another industrial colossus.

The most exclusive Jaguar road car of all time was the XK-SS of 1957. This was a slightly modified D-Type race car, and only eighteen such cars were originally produced.

E-TYPE AND MARK 2: THE CARS THAT CHANGED JAGUAR

THE YEARS FROM 1958 to 1966 were a period of great activity for Jaguar: many new models were launched; other businesses were acquired; sales and production were constantly expanding; and, behind the scenes, Sir William was discreetly searching for a successor for the day when he finally decided to step down and reluctantly retire.

Although cars such as the sensational E-Type and the best-selling Mark 2 range have their own stories, it was the company's relentless expansion that governed their launch, and the ability to have them made and sold. We must therefore consider the takeovers before we can describe the new cars.

Not only did Jaguar need more space in which to build its cars, but Sir William also had ambitions to turn Jaguar into a compact automotive empire. Subject to the availability of finance (and although Jaguar was a public company, Sir William and his family still held the majority shareholding), he therefore set out on such a quest in 1960.

The same year, he bought the Daimler company from BSA; not only was Daimler a prestigious car-maker with a big factory in the Radford district of Coventry, but it was also producing single- and double-decker buses, and even military vehicles such as the Ferret armoured car. At a stroke, therefore, the Jaguar company doubled in size, with a total workforce approaching eight thousand, and it was not long before all Jaguar engine and transmission manufacture and assembly were concentrated on the Daimler site.

Next, the Wolverhampton-based truck company, Guy, was absorbed, shortly to be followed by Meadows, which specialised in making heavy commercial vehicle engines. Jaguar then considered taking over the fledgling Lotus company (which was apparently on offer, though no company took control of it for another twenty-five years), before going for one final, glamorous purchase, that of Coventry-Climax, also based in Coventry.

Although Coventry-Climax's 'bread and butter' came from making forklift trucks for industry, and a variety of small industrial engines, the glamour came from its limited production of high-performance light-alloy

Opposite:
For years, Jaguar's principal problem with the E-Type was not in selling the cars, but in producing enough to keep up with the demand. This was Browns Lane in 1967.

power units – the FWA/FWE series – for sale to several small and independent car-makers such as Lotus, TVR, Turner and Cooper, and from its involvement in Formula One.

At that time Coventry-Climax F1 engines were winning at every level (particularly in Lotuses driven by Jim Clark), and although Sir William was not enthusiastic about the cost of these ventures, he welcomed the positive publicity that they brought. Furthermore, the company's technical chief, Walter Hassan, had spent many years at Jaguar, and he was speedily brought back to Browns Lane to relieve the pressure on Bill Heynes in the engine-design department.

Only in this ambitious and corporate atmosphere could Jaguar even consider going ahead with an ambitious product expansion plan for the 1960s, and it was not surprising that there was no place for an on-going motor-sport programme within the company at the same time. In the first half of the 1960s, not only did the company launch new E-Type, Mark 2, Mark X, and spin-off models, but there were new products at Daimler (both cars and buses), work on new trucks at Guy, and a proposed joint enterprise with Cummins of the United States, makers of massive diesel engines for trucks, though this last did not come to maturity.

The original Mark I car was restyled and much improved in 1959, when it became the Mark 2, complete with different window styling, and with a wider choice of engines.

On the other hand, Coventry-Climax was gradually, but decisively, pulled out of motor sport, and would never return. Although the 1½-litre V8 continued to be a race-winning power unit in Formula One until the end of 1965, a proposed flat-sixteen replacement was not a success and was speedily cancelled.

As would eventually be revealed, the biggest design and development programme in the group at this time (and Jaguar must be considered as a group from this moment on) was to finalise what became known as the Mark 2 compact saloon, get it on sale in 1959, and then knuckle down to mould it into a vast array of derivatives. This was done in a typically pragmatic manner, first of all by Sir William completely revisiting the Mark 1 style, changing the window layout, widening the rear track, and making sure that all the existing XK engines (2.4-, 3.4- and the newly developed 3.8-litre sizes) were made available.

Although annual Jaguar sales rose above twenty thousand for the first time, this was only the beginning, for in the next few years the Mark 2 range would expand to include a Daimler version, complete with the existing Daimler V8 engine, a more advanced long-tail derivative called the S-Type, which had independent rear suspension, and finally the 420, which was even more high-tech, but with altered front-end styling.

3.8-litre-engined Mark 2s were potential race-winners all around the world in the first years of the 1960s. This machine is competing in the Tour de France.

The styling of the Mark 2 range was unmistakable. Many cars sold to export markets were equipped, like this one, with white-wall tyres and chrome wire-spoke wheels.

Opposite: Although Sir William Lyons was justly proud of the E-Type, which was first revealed in 1961, he had little to do with the style of the car. It was partly an evolution of the D-Type's shape, and partly the product of aerodynamic studies by his specialist, Malcolm Sayer.

This, on its own, would have been enough to keep Jaguar dealerships busy all round the world (and particularly in North America, where the 125-mph 3.8-litre Mark 2 was proving to be very popular), but it was the arrival of the amazingly sleek and fast E-Type in 1961 that made the headlines. This was a car that had started out as a racing sports-car project, intended to take over from the world-famous D-Type on circuits from Le Mans to Sebring, Florida, but which had been refined, enlarged and re-engineered during development.

Now, instead of going racing, it was meant to run in the streets of the world's cities, as the XK150 was already doing, though the E-Type now had the potential to reach nearly 150 mph, making it one of the fastest cars in the world. The original racing intent explains why it had such an advanced chassis – the combination of a multi-tubular front end, allied to a monocoque body tub, all-round independent suspension (by torsion bars at the front, and coil springs at the rear), and four-wheel disc brakes.

Although the original 3.8-litre E-Types had several problems with design, development and build quality when new, these were mostly forgiven by an adoring public, especially those in the United Kingdom, who could buy one for no more than £2,098. One motoring writer of mature years said that he knew it would be a worldwide success when he found that pretty girls started smiling at even him when he drove one.

So, when a new model was as sexy as this, what did it matter if there was not quite enough space inside the cabin (it had, after all, been shaped around the compact figure of chief test driver Norman Dewis), that the heating system was by no means state-of-the-art, or that it was possible for an early model to overheat in city traffic? The seductive, wind-tunnel-inspired shape was unlike that of any other road car, the 265-bhp engine promised

When it was
introduced in
1961, the E-Type
was an instant
sensation, for no
other car in the
world offered
looks like this, and
a top speed of
nearly 150 mph,
at such a low
price.

The E-Type,
particularly in
fixed-head coupé
form, looked
stunning from any
angle, especially
from overhead.

colossal open-road performance, and the car was uniquely attractive, both visually and in driving appeal.

Like the XKs that had gone before it, the E-Type outsold all its makers' original forecasts and was soon selling at the rate of five to six thousand cars a year. Open-top, fast-back coupé and even stretched 2+2 versions were all available, making the cars irresistible. All versions of the E-Type would remain on the market for fifteen years, and more than 72,000 would be sold.

With the E-Type and the Mark 2 making the headlines, it was surprising that Jaguar found time to replace the long-running Mark VII/VIII/IX range in 1961 with the massive unit-construction Mark X. As a direct replacement for the old car, this was a huge machine intended to appeal to export markets (and particularly to North America), which explains why it ran on a 120-inch wheelbase and was both wider and longer than any Jaguar produced before or since.

Even though Bill Heynes's engineers did their best to mix and match the running gear from everything else that was coming along in other new Jaguars – the Mark X used the same engine as the E-Type, and the same independent rear suspension as the E-Type and the forthcoming S-Type

The Mark X, Jaguar's largest ever car, was introduced in 1961. Here is a line-up of the cars, waiting to be completed at Browns Lane.

saloon – it was the colossal bodyshell (for this was a true six-seater) that made it unique in Britain. Sir William had spent so long on working up the styling of this car, which had originally been intended as a Mark IX, that it became known as the 'Mark Time' by his staff (though never to his face) before it finally made its way through the workshops. Nevertheless, it was as elegant as current trends, and his sales staff's recommendations, would allow.

By 1963 the company had spent so much on new model development that for the next few seasons at least it would have to rely on improvements, and 'gap-filling', rather than innovation, to keep up the demand. Production soon topped out at about 25,000, of which ten thousand cars were exported, about four thousand of those going to North America. Even so, Jaguar watchers had to stay alert if they were to keep up with the changes brought in, seemingly every year, until the mid-1960s.

This Mark X is posed in front of the Forth Road Bridge in Scotland.

First, Sir William had to sort out what he had inherited at Daimler. Not only was there the challenge of turning the oddly styled new SP250 sports car into a reliable product (with a glass-fibre body, which was none too rigid, there were build-quality issues to be resolved), but a new flagship model, the 4½-litre V8-engined Majestic Major, had to be marketed. Most important of all was that a Jaguar-based saloon, the 2½-litre, complete with a neat and powerful 140-bhp 2.5-litre V8 engine, was also put on sale, this becoming the first Daimler to be assembled in the main Jaguar factory. The larger Daimler V8 engine was also tested in Jaguar's Mark X saloon, which proved to be even faster than had been hoped, but, as it was not an engine that could be produced in large quantities, that particular project had to be dropped.

In the meantime, Sir William and his technical chief, Bill Heynes, carried on wringing every possible advantage out of their big investment in existing models. First was the arrival of the S-Type, which, although closely based on the Mark 2 saloon, featured a lengthened and rather squared-up tail, coil-spring independent rear suspension like that of the E-Type, the larger of the XK engines, and a more completely kitted-out interior. This car carried on alongside the Mark 2 for the next five years.

Next came the launch of several evolutionary models that benefited from two major mechanical developments: the 4.2-litre XK engine (this was to be the final 'stretch' of a much-loved power unit), and an all-synchromesh manual gearbox. Both had been under development at Browns Lane for some time, and both would bring real improvement to the cars to which they were applied: in 4.2-litre form, not only was the latest and still maturing E-Type a better and more flexible machine than before, but so was the Mark X saloon.

The big engine would not immediately find a home in the Mark 2 and S-Type saloons, though the gearboxes would, as Sir William had more innovation in mind for Jaguar's near future. Not only did he spend ages styling the third, and final, derivative of the Mark 2, the 420, for launch in 1966, but he also approved the launch of a bigger, longer-wheelbase, 'family' E-Type – the 2+2.

Clearly this was a strategy that worked, for Jaguar's annual production was now approaching thirty thousand, more cars were now being exported than were staying at home, and Sir William was actively looking to secure his succession, and the future of his company. Suddenly, in 1966, he astonished everyone – even, it is said, his closest colleagues, to whom he did not confide his strategy – by announcing that he would merge the Jaguar Group with the British Motor Corporation (BMC). This, the foundation of British Motor Holdings, was the start of the process that led to the birth of British Leyland in 1968.

From a heritage of inspired design and engineering, comes the best Jaguar ever built.

They are some of the most coveted automobiles of all time. The 1961 E-type. The 1954 XK-140. The 1936 SS-100—automobiles that created the indelible tradition of Jaguar design and engineering excellence. Today, that tradition is carried forward by the 1992 XJS.

Through the years, Jaguar has pioneered technological innovations such as monocoque construction, four-wheel disc brakes, and fully independent suspension—achievements reflected today in the best sporting Jaguar ever built.

Now, computers and robotics are part of a highly advanced manufacturing process. New quality assurance procedures and sophisticated electronic controls exist side-by-side with the time-honored art of handcrafting wood and leather.

For its owner, the reward is a car of sensuous beauty and enviable performance. Its interior is an environment of unparalleled luxury and convenience. Race-bred handling and agile response create a relationship between driver and car at once confident and exhilirating.

And for 1992, even Jaguar's warranty has been enhanced, to four yea' 50,000 miles. For the nearest dealer, who can provide details on the limite warranty and Jaguar Royal Charter Care, call 1-800-4-JAGUAR.

J A G U A I

XJ6, V12 ENGINES AND BRITISH LEYLAND

FROM 1966, when Jaguar joined forces with BMC, until 1984, when it broke free from the corporate wreckage of the nationalised British Leyland to become independent once again, the company had a turbulent existence. Although the brand survived, the clientele stayed loyal, and the cars were always fast, stylish and stimulating, there were times when the future looked very doubtful indeed.

When Jaguar joined up with BMC to form BMH, it lost much of its ability to plan for its own future. First, more or less at the British government's insistence, BMH linked up with Leyland in 1968 to form British Leyland. That colossus, which originally included brands as disparate as Jaguar and MG, Triumph and AEC trucks, Austin and Scammell, suffered seven years of corporate, financial and industrial relations strife before having to be 'rescued' (in other words taken into state ownership) in 1975.

As the government then applied more and more policies that tended to render famous brands nameless (and powerless), Jaguar gradually lost individuality, and finally the Browns Lane premises became known merely as the 'British Leyland Large Car Plant'. Even so, in the six years that remained for Sir William Lyons, who finally elected to retire soon after he had reached his seventieth birthday in 1971, he made sure that he would always be one of the most important and powerful executives in the corporation, and that by his every action Jaguar would hang on to its independence.

In those years, although almost every action – public and private – of British Leyland tended to be chaotic rather than logical, Sir William ensured that Jaguar's product policy, and its development, would be independent of most influences. Even before BMH had been founded in 1966, he had laid the foundations for Jaguar's short- and medium-term future – the plan being to evolve a versatile family of saloon and sporty cars, allied to the birth of a brand-new V12 engine.

He also kept a careful eye on what the other brands within the corporation were doing and wanted to do. In particular, it was Sir William who saw to the killing off of a putative Rover executive saloon (coded P8),

Opposite:
Even after its final restyling, the XJS was still selling well, and needed only high-quality advertising to keep it in the public eye.

37

Opposite page: To sell the XJ6, Jaguar always made much of its unique specification and appearance.

The long-running XJ6 range made its debut in 1968 and ran, in one type or another, for the next twenty-four years. This was 'Job 1', the first example completed.

and an extremely promising Rover sports car project (P6B/P9) – both of which might have harmed various Jaguar programmes. On the other hand, he also made sure that where Jaguar needed funds, and other resources, to bring his new products to the market place, it would get them, while being careful to preserve Jaguar, Daimler, Radford and Browns Lane as his personal technical and commercial empire.

First seen in 1968, the carefully styled, engineered and developed XJ6 was central to all those plans. Not only did this car, which had a completely new chassis/platform, but which retained the XK engine and the associated running gear, eventually replace every single one of Jaguar's (and Daimler's) existing saloons, but it was also the foundation of a sporty car that would take over from the E-Type in the mid-1970s.

The wait had definitely been worthwhile. In came the XJ6, and within a year out went all the Mark 2-based cars, the S-Type, the 420, and the 420G (which was what the Mark X had latterly been called). Browns Lane had never been at the cutting edge of production technology, but this made it easier to build just one basic car, whose assembly lines could now wind their way in and out of the congested halls.

Everything about the XJ6 family – except, admittedly, the build quality, which sometimes depended on products supplied by Britain's complacent components industry, and on the mood of an increasingly militant British Leyland workforce – was right. Visually it was stunning, for it offered more refinement, more elegance and more versatile accommodation than any

previous Jaguar. It was no wonder that by the time the very last of all the saloon derivatives – V12-engined cars – were produced in 1992, no fewer than 404,000 of all types had been produced.

To a world filled with compromise, we make no contribution.

Which may suggest why the Jaguar XJ6 was selected as one of the world's ten best cars by Road & Track.

All cars begin as an idea. The Jaguar XJ6 began as an almost impossible idea.

It was to design a sedan that would set new standards of comfort and luxury, road-holding and ride, steering and braking, performance and safety, while maintaining the standard of value traditionally associated with Jaguar.

In building the Jaguar XJ6, we held fast to that idea without compromise.

A few particulars.

The XJ6 is powered by a 4.2 litre twin-overhead camshaft engine that was described by a prominent automotive publication as "almost faultless".

Motor Trend described its handling in one word: "superb".

That characteristic derives from the engineering that went into the Jaguar XJ6. A fully-independent 4-wheel suspension system designed to negotiate the ruts and bumps of English country roads.

And power-assisted rack-and-pinion steering. Caliper-type disc brakes front and rear, also power-assisted.

In naming the Jaguar XJ6 as one of the world's ten best cars of 1971, *Road & Track* wrote, "When we first drove the XJ6

we said it was 'uncannily swift, gloriously silent and safe as houses.' We still like that description. It was also one of the best-handling sedans in the world as well..."

Jaguar XJ6: an idea that became reality without compromise.

For the name of your nearest Jaguar dealer and for information about overseas delivery, dial (800) 631-1972 except in New Jersey where the number is (800) 962-2803. Calls are toll-free.

BRITISH LEYLAND MOTORS INC., LEONIA, NEW JERSEY 07605

Jaguar

With annual production gradually creeping up to more than thirty thousand cars a year – that figure was passed, for the first time, in 1969/70 – the XJ6 seemed to be right for every market, particularly in North America. American buyers enjoyed making and circulating the usual jokes (of the sometimes troublesome air conditioning, it was once suggested that rich Texans should buy two cars at once, one of them to be kept in a drive-in freezer to keep it cold), but they carried on buying.

XJ6s gradually changed, and improved, over the years, with the Series II appearing in 1973, the Series III (with styling retouched by Pininfarina) in 1979, with 2.8-litre, 3.4-litre and 4.2-litre engines, and with Daimler Sovereign types also appearing alongside, and in the same showrooms. The sleek two-door coupé version went on sale in 1975 but was never a big seller, though fuel-injected engines made more of an impact when North American exhaust emission rules made them desirable.

In the meantime the company had patiently been developing an all-new engine – a magnificent 5.3-litre V12 power unit – and was ready to

Series II XJ6s came along in 1973, with minor style changes, but with a much enhanced specification.

launch it in 1971. It was only the second new engine produced by Jaguar since 1945, but it was to have a long and glittering career, not only in saloons and limousines, but in sports cars, coupés, and in race cars of the 1980s and 1990s.

The first prototype V12s were 5-litre units with twin-overhead-camshaft cylinder heads, and might once have been used in race cars such as the abandoned XJ13 project, but the series production road-car unit (which would always be produced at what had been the Daimler factory at Radford) had single-cam heads, was incredibly smooth, silent and refined, and would be criticised only for its heavy fuel consumption. Although the V12 was never intended to replace the XK engine – the AJ6 family that followed in the 1980s would do that – it broadened an altogether extensive range and inspired respect from Jaguar's admirers.

V12-engined Jaguars proliferated in the 1970s. First there was the E-Type Series III, which was finally retired in 1975; then there was the XJ12 saloon (Jaguar had made sure that this engine would just – if only just – squeeze into the engine bay of the XJ6), the Daimler Double Six version of that car, and ultimately the XJ-S sports coupé. All were capable of 150 mph, and all had startling qualities as astonishingly flexible road cars.

In the meantime, Sir William Lyons's long-forecast retirement finally took place in 1972, his final major achievements having been to see the V12 engine launched, and to see the style of the still secret XJ-S coupé moving towards maturity. Technical chief Bill Heynes had already retired, and so

During the 1960s, Jaguar built just one example of a proposed mid-engined race car, the XJ13, which had an early type of 60-degree V12 engine fitted, and which produced 500 bhp.

F. R. W. ('Lofty') England, who had been groomed for this job for some years, took over from Sir William as Jaguar's chairman, with Bob Knight (mechanical) and Walter Hassan (engines and transmissions) taking over from Heynes.

England, however, was not content in this new position for long, as British Leyland internal politics, and its troubled labour relations problems, made his task very difficult. Less than two years after his appointment, therefore, he resigned, and British Leyland's chairman, Lord Stokes, imposed a new 'Leyland' man, Geoffrey Robinson, in his place. 'Lofty' England went to live in Austria, where he became a much respected Jaguar heritage specialist for the next twenty years. Robinson's tenure was short, as he was eased out by the British Leyland board soon after it was nationalised – after which he went on to become a controversial Labour politician and industrialist.

The third derivative of the E-Type, the Series III, complete with the new 5.3-litre V12 engine, was announced in 1971 and was built until 1974/5.

The mid- and late-1970s presented quite a challenge for Jaguar. The energy crisis of 1973–4 (and the subsequent steep rise in fuel prices) hit hard at the makers of thirsty and high-performance cars. As a consequence, British Leyland, the parent company in this conglomerate, struck serious financial trouble at the end of 1974 and had to be rescued – effectively nationalised – by the government of the day. A government nominee, Lord Ryder, became the company's new chairman, many previous British Leyland directors, including Lord Stokes and Geoffrey Robinson, were eased out, and Jaguar became in effect no more than a small part of the 'Leyland Cars' grouping.

This was the period, too, when the long-running E-Type was finally retired. Jaguar was so proud of this model that it kept the very last example

ever made, which remains in the company's heritage collection to this day. No new model could ever directly replace such a celebrated machine. However, the sporty new Jaguar that effectively took its place used the same type of V12 engine, but was based on a shortened version of the XJ6/XJ12's platform. It was sold only as a closed coupe at first, and was a larger car than the E-Type had ever been. Even though the styling had been started by Sir William Lyons before he retired, the looks of the car were controversial, and remain so to this day.

Because of the shambolic fortunes of the nationalised British Leyland, of which it was a part, the late 1970s were a very difficult time for Jaguar. Poor labour relations, frequent and damaging strikes, allied to unacceptably high

The XJ-S was based on a shortened version of the XJ12's platform, with this unique style, complete with the controversial 'flying buttresses' on the rear quarters.

The last Series III E-Type was built in 1974, though not put on show until 1975, and has been preserved by Jaguar as part of its heritage fleet.

inflation, hit hard at sales. The charismatic Michael Edwardes became the chairman of the corporation at the end of 1977, but an enforced link to Rover and Triumph that he initiated did not help; the XJ-S had its own sales problems in the United States – for a time, production of the XJ-S was suspended to balance stocks – and in the end it was only a series of drastic measures which saved the Jaguar brand.

One of these was that an ambitious young executive, John Egan (then working at Massey-Ferguson, in Coventry), was appointed chairman, and the second was that as a consequence – belatedly, but just in time to make a difference – the company got to grips with its problems, and the atmosphere soon lightened. It was a gradual process, but a combination of new technology in the V12 engine (this was the 'HE', or High Efficiency, tune-up), a rapid improvement in the way bodies were built by Jaguar's body-production plant at Castle Bromwich, near Birmingham, and the sheer enthusiasm of almost everyone in the business, soon made Jaguars seem fashionable, exciting and desirable again.

From 1983 the XJ-S got a new lease of life, not only by acquiring an additional body style – the smart Cabriolet, which was the first open-top version to appear – but also by becoming the first to use the new-generation AJ6 engine, which had been under development for some years at Browns Lane. This engine was critical to Jaguar's future, for it was meant to replace the old XK power unit, by being smaller, lighter and more fuel-efficient: it was all of those, and was also earmarked for use in new saloons, which were already on the way.

In 1984, however, there was more to make life, and the future, look exciting for every Jaguar customer, watcher and enthusiast. In 1979, at the General Election, Britain's electorate had voted in a new Conservative administration. Margaret Thatcher was the new Prime Minister, and her mission was to privatise as many of the nation's unwanted assets as possible. Jaguar, having lived under the shadow of British Leyland for a decade, was earmarked for sale, and found a ready market.

After Sir William Lyons had retired, Jaguar took outside advice on its styling, hiring Pininfarina of Italy to retouch the XJ6. This resulted in the Series III car of 1979.

MOTOR RACING FROM
THE 1950s TO THE 1990s

STARTING IN 1951, with an emphatic victory in the Le Mans 24 Hour race, Jaguar became a successful participant in motor sport. With specialised sports cars, then with racing saloons, and for a time with dedicated Formula One cars, the brand was usually present, and successful, at the very top level. The costs – of designing, building and campaigning cars – which were always high, eventually became astronomical, but in almost every case the results achieved seemed to make the expense worthwhile.

It all began with the XK120C, affectionately known as the 'C-Type' by its many followers, which started the trend of using as many Jaguar production-based components as possible. Though the body shape (by Malcolm Sayer) and the chassis design (by Bob Knight) of this two-seater were both special, much of what was hidden away had started life in the XK120 road car. With 200 bhp from the XK engine at the beginning, and with 220 bhp in maturity, the C-Type soon had disc brakes added to its chassis, and, with a 150-mph top speed, was good enough to win the Le Mans 24 Hour race twice, in 1951 and 1953.

Its successor was the legendary D-Type, which was beautifully shaped, more powerful (250 bhp, rising to more than 290 bhp with fuel injection in later years), smaller, lighter, and technically more complex. It had a potential top speed of 175 mph and won the Le Mans race in 1955, 1956 and 1957, also achieving great victories in endurance events at circuits such as Sebring in Florida. It became one of Jaguar's great icons, still worshipped in the 'classic' movement, and commanding incredibly high prices when sold at auction.

It was typical that Sir William took every possible commercial advantage from these factory programmes, for he laid down rudimentary, but real, production lines at Browns Lane for each type, going on to sell more than fifty C-Types, more than seventy D-Types, and in 1957 they even sold eighteen of the super-exclusive XKSS, which was the trimmed and slightly civilised road-car version of the D-Type. More would undoubtedly have followed if the facilities had not been consumed in the fire of February 1957.

Opposite: Amazingly, this massive Mark VII was good enough to win the wintry Monte Carlo Rally in Ronnie Adams's hands in 1956. The very same car was also used as a successful circuit-racing machine in British touring car events.

'Lofty' England (left) became Jaguar's service manager in the 1950s, and also became the manager of the race team at that time. He is seen with Sir William Lyons.

Jaguar won the first of many Le Mans victories in 1951 with this C-Type, here seen streaming away from the start of the 24 Hour race.

Jaguar developed the D-Type as a racing sports car, which went on to win the Le Mans 24 Hour race in 1955, 1956 and 1957, along with many other races in many countries.

In the meantime, the company's road cars not only began to record victory after victory in international rallies (Ian Appleyard's XK120, NUB 120, was the most famous of all in Europe, but Ronnie Adams's Mark VII victory in the Monte Carlo Rally of 1956 ran him close), but the saloons also won production car races wherever the regulations allowed them. At first, it was the big works Mark VIIs that outpaced the rest of the world; then the 3.8-litre Mark 2s took over, not only in the United Kingdom and United States, but in Europe and Australia too.

Ian Appleyard's famous XK120, NUB 120, was the most distinguished of all Jaguar rally cars, and won many major events in three years.

49

From 1951 to the mid-1960s it seemed that no other make of car could beat them, and the Jaguar factory, notably the engine development areas, the service department managed by 'Lofty' England, and discreet little corners of the engineering offices, made sure that they were as fast and, most importantly, as reliable, as possible.

Although, as already described, the E-Type made its name and its reputation as a wonderfully charismatic road car, we must also remember that it originated in 1957 as a race-car project, when a small 2.4-litre two-seater seemed set fair to take over from the D-Types. Over time, though, and excepting a 1960 Le Mans entry for the E2A prototype, the E-Type was scarcely raced. Much-modified road cars shone on the circuits in 1961, and the extremely rare (thirteen cars built) 'lightweights' looked promising, but the company was never able to get back into motor racing in a big way.

There was, however, one serious (though clandestine) project in the mid-1960s, when the first of the big V12 engines (then with twin-cam heads per

As raced in the United States in the late 1970s, the Group 44 XJR5 greatly enhanced the model's reputation.

cylinder bank) was completed and installed in a mid-engined two-seater chassis, known as XJ13. If the potential cost of competing against Ferrari, Porsche and Ford had not become so horrendous, and if Jaguar had not become a part of British Leyland, where such programmes were then frowned on, this could have been a serious contender, for it not only looked splendid, but was capable of at least 200 mph. Only one car was built, and survives to this day, though several replicas have been constructed by wealthy private individuals in modern times.

There was then a lull until the mid-1970s, when British Leyland/Leyland Cars again decided to embrace motor sport and hired Broadspeed to develop massively powerful (600-bhp) versions of the XJ12C coupé for international saloon-car racing. Complete with their patriotic red, blue and white colour scheme, the cars looked magnificent in 1976 and 1977, but they were not quite quick enough to win major events.

Soon after this, attention turned to the V12-engined XJ-S, which was altogether smaller, lighter and potentially more suitable than the XJ12C. First in the United States, where Bob Tullius's Group 44 cars won many races and championships, and then from 1982 in Europe, where Tom Walkinshaw's TWR-prepared cars became the dominant cars in worldwide 'touring car' racing (because the XJ-S was just about a four-seater, it qualified as a 'saloon'

Tom Walkinshaw's TWR concern turned the XJ-S into a formidably successful 'saloon' car racer in the 1980s, winning the European Touring Car Championship before the team turned to specialised race cars.

51

– according to the regulations and the dimensions of the cabin), the XJ-S proved that it could win anywhere, in any circuit or weather conditions.

In 1983 there were five victories in the European Touring Car Championship; then in 1984 a three-car team took the twelve-event championship outright, with Walkinshaw himself nominated as the winning driver. The V12 engine was powerful and reliable, the cars handled better than their size and bulk had ever originally promised, and it was only the arrival of yet more specialised Jaguar race cars – the XJR series – which made them obsolete.

Two separate mid-V12-engined racing sports car programmes dominated Jaguar's sporting efforts for the rest of the 1980s, the American effort being led by Tullius's Group 44 team, and the European effort by Walkinshaw's TWR organisation. Except for one foray to the Le Mans 24 Hour race in 1985, the Group 44 effort was confined to North America.

XJR-5s and XJR-7s won many races from 1985 to 1987, but from 1988 TWR/Jaguar took over the North American programme, developing the XJR-9 GTP. This was swiftly supplanted by the XJR-10, which ran with a TWR turbocharged V6 engine that engineers had evolved from the MG Metro 6R4 rally car project (a much 'productionised' version of that engine would eventually be used in the XJ220 road car).

It was the World Championship programme, however, which made the most headlines. XJR6s established a successful dynasty in 1986, soon having 690 bhp from TWR-developed 6.5-litre versions of the V12, but it was the adoption of the lurid mauve-and-white livery of the Silk Cut cigarette sponsorship that made the latest XJR-8 cars (now with 7.0-litre/720-bhp engines) startling. Eight outright victories and the World Championship made

Opposite top:
Not only was the XJ220 a stunning road car, but it was also a useful race car in events that suited its capacity and size.

Opposite bottom:
The first of the 'Silk Cut' Jaguar successes at Le Mans came in 1988, when this XJR9 won in fine style.

TWR won the prestigious Le Mans 24 Hour race for the second time in 1990, using this 720-bhp 7.0-litre V12-engined XJR12.

them the dominant brand in sports-car racing, and this record was surpassed in 1988 when the team (now using XJR-9s) won the Le Mans 24 Hour race as well a second World Championship.

By 1990 the TWR race programme was so serious that they used turbo-V6 XJR-11s for most races, but reverted to a related XJR-12, complete with 7.0-litre Jaguar V12 engine, for Le Mans. It was an extremely wise decision

(especially as a new owner, Ford, was paying all the bills for its new subsidiary), for two of the four team cars finished the race in first and second places, with Martin Brundle, John Neilsen and Price Cobb sharing the winning car. Again, this time with much help from Walkinshaw's expert crew, Jaguar had demonstrated how good they could be in long-distance motor racing.

Nor was this the end – though it was for Jaguar-engined race cars. For 1991, in one last fling at the much changed World Sports Car Championship, TWR developed the new XJR-14, which was smaller and lighter, but just as effective as before. This time, because the regulations required it, the team had to use a smaller, normally aspirated engine. Accordingly Ford made it possible for 700-bhp 3.5-litre V8 Cosworth HBs (their current Formula One engine, as used in Benettons, for instance) to be available. Jaguar/TWR celebrated this by developing the dominant racing sports car of the year, and easily won yet another World Championship. It was a wonderful way to bring this programme to a close.

So-called 'Jaguars' appeared in Formula One in the early 2000s, but this was little more than a rebadging exercise for cars sponsored by Ford. Originally, there had been Stewart (after Jackie Stewart) F1 cars powered by Cosworth V10 engines; then Stewart had sold out to Ford, and suddenly, with publicity rather than engineering in mind, a 'Jaguar' F1 car was born. However, the cars, which were built and maintained in Milton Keynes, were not a short-term success, so that at the end of 2004 Ford sold the business to Red Bull.

Opposite page: Four generations of specialised race or prototype supercars (from front to rear): the C-Type, the D-Type, the XJ13 prototype, and the mid-engined XJ220.

The Jaguar brand appeared in Formula One for a few seasons in the 2000s, but these cars were built outside the factory and were powered by Ford-Cosworth V10 engines.

INDEPENDENCE,
FORD, LAND ROVER
AND TATA

No sooner had the company been floated on the Stock Exchange in mid-1984 than a wave of optimism grew up among Jaguar supporters, staff and enthusiasts. Everything, it seemed, would now be possible. The company, for sure, was well placed, with fine managers, good engineers, and plans for the future. The new boss, John Egan, knew exactly what he wanted to do – but had to come to terms with the fact that he had only limited financial resources.

So far as the public was concerned, the company ploughed ahead, not only by launching the long-awaited new-generation XJ6 in 1986 (this was always coded 'XJ40' within the company), but also by commissioning a fine new design and development complex in another part of Coventry, and then by launching the XJ-S Convertible. Sales rose, as did the company's reputation – but the need for more funds became urgent.

The only way the problem could be solved, it seemed, was for Jaguar to get together again with a larger and more prosperous grouping. This time, though, it would not be a forced union. Discreetly at first, but less so as the

weeks passed, company advisers let it be known that Jaguar was on the market. Eventually, and after a bidding battle between General Motors and Ford, in the autumn of 1989 it was Ford which paid approximately £1.6 billion to take complete control.

Almost from this point, and certainly as the next two decades proceeded, Jaguar was progressively dominated by its new owner – benevolently in almost every way, but it was definitely subservient to corporate whims and fancies. When Ford managers arrived and swept through the factories, their first reaction was that much modernisation was needed – and they made haste to finance such changes. Furthermore, the pace of technical change, and of the introduction of new products, accelerated.

First, approval came for the magnificent 215-mph XJ220 supercar, which was engineered under Tom Walkinshaw's control, used a modified version of the turbocharged racing V6 engine, and was to be built at a new small factory near Banbury. Only 350 were planned, but in the end just 271 were sold, for the classic car boom faltered at this time, and many so-called enthusiasts (in some cases, actually 'investors') cancelled their orders.

Next the XJ-S, of which ten thousand were being built every year, benefited from a major late-term facelift, not only around the rear style, but in terms of upgraded engines. That launch came in 1991, and kept the car

Two extremes of 'Jaguar': an original-type Swallow sidecar posed alongside a 540-bhp mid-engined XJ220 supercar.

going to 1996 (up to when more than 115,000 XJ-Ss of all types had been built). It was then replaced by the altogether smoother, and less controversially styled, XK8.

The major innovation of this period, however, was the spending of huge amounts of money on the Castle Bromwich factory, where every Jaguar bodyshell was produced, and preparing it for several new generations of saloon car to be made there. Ford then approved the launch of an all-new V8 engine (which would be revealed in 1996), for which they provided production facilities at a massive Ford factory at Bridgend in South Wales. In the meantime there was also a much revised 'XJ40' car to be launched with sleeker front and rear styling (Sir William would surely have approved), and then, in the autumn of 1998, the appearance of a new Jaguar S-Type saloon.

Here was real evidence of Ford's corporate approach to Jaguar, for the entire platform, and much of the S-Type's superstructure and body style, were shared with a Ford-USA model to be named the Lincoln LS. As well as the modern Jaguar V8 engine, there was also to be a 3-litre V6-engined version of the car, that engine being a modified version of a Ford engine that was in use in many countries and models.

First used in the XK8 sports car, the original and all-new V8 engine made its debut in 1996, and still powered a variety of Jaguars, Land Rovers and Range Rovers in the early 2010s.

Five generations of Jaguar sports cars, covering more than sixty years (clockwise from left): SS100, XK120, E-Type, XJ-S, and XK8.

Then came the next shock, for BMW (which had taken over the rump of the Rover Group in 1994) then decided to rid itself of that troublesome business, and among other things sold off Land Rover to Ford. That company's 'master plan' soon took shape, in that Ford would soon arrange to use Jaguar V8 engines in the larger Land Rover models, such as the Discovery and the Range Rover, and from there it was only a small corporate step to arrange to use a newly developed turbocharged V6 diesel engine (originally of 2.7 litres, but later of 3.0 litres) in all these models. Shortly, this unit was applied to the S-Type, and proceeded to sell very briskly indeed. The financial press soon learned to discuss Jaguar-Land-Rover as a single corporate unit, for the two managements henceforth operated increasingly closely together.

The original S-Type was launched in 1998 and shared much of its design architecture with a Ford-owned Lincoln from the United States. Its platform was later used under the XF.

In the meantime Ford had financed the development of the X-Type, the 'small' Jaguar, which proved to be controversial throughout its ten-year career. Launched in 2001, and assembled at a former Ford factory at Halewood, near Liverpool, it was unashamedly based on the platform of the Ford Mondeo, but also enjoyed an intriguing product mix of Jaguar innovations – transverse-mounted engines, front-wheel drive on some versions and four-wheel drive on others, a Ford-based diesel engine eventually, and an estate-car alternative. V6-engined versions were fast and

satisfying, but lower-powered types sometimes disappointed. The X-Type helped annual Jaguar sales to reach 100,000 for the first time – but not as high as expected.

For the next few years, however, Ford-influenced launches followed in quick succession. First there was the new-generation XJ6 of 2003, which looked very similar to the car it replaced. Then came the second-generation XK8 (looking almost like the previous car) in 2005. This, though, was small-scale news compared with Ford's eventual decision to abandon the Browns Lane site in 2005, and to concentrate all its future assembly facilities at a much expanded Castle Bromwich factory.

It was there that the next two major launches took place – both of them relatively conventional in engineering, with front engines and rear-wheel drive, but both startlingly beautiful, with fast-back styling of which Sir William would certainly have been proud. The XF of 2008 took over from the S-Type (but retained that car's platform and basic running gear), while the new XJ of 2010 replaced the previous XJ, which had enjoyed a rather anonymous career of only seven years.

The biggest surprise, though, had already happened, for as Ford's operations came under pressure, and its policies changed, it decided to sell off Jaguar-Land-Rover, and found that the Indian conglomerate Tata was a very willing purchaser. That was in 2008; Tata apparently paid £1.5 billion for the business, and immediately began reshaping Jaguar-Land-Rover to its own worldwide concepts. With Jaguar, as a brand, now approaching its eightieth birthday, the company seemed to be as well-founded as ever, and the future looked very exciting.

The X-Type was in production from 2001 to 2010. Some versions had four-wheel drive, and some were diesel-powered, both these being innovations for Jaguar.

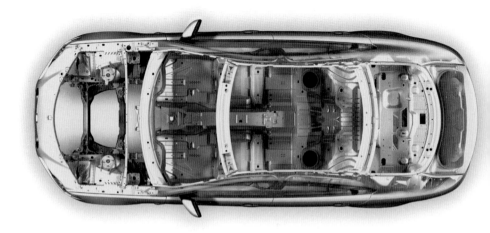

Below: The XF was introduced in 2007, showing off Jaguar's new style direction, and showcasing the Castle Bromwich factory, where such cars were to be built in the future.

Above: This was the way that Jaguar chose to emphasise the high-tech body structure of the new XF, which used elements of the previous S-Type in its make-up.

FURTHER INFORMATION

FURTHER READING

Porter, Philip, and Skilleter, Paul. *Sir William Lyons, The Official Biography*. Haynes, 1980.

Whyte, Andrew. *Jaguar – The Definitive History of a Great British Car*. Haynes, fourth edition 1994.

In addition, there are many books covering the story of individual models and specific ranges.

CLUBS

All round the world, there are dozens of clubs that look after the interests and preservation of the Jaguar marque. The author recommends the use of an Internet search engine to locate them. The principal British clubs are:

Jaguar Drivers' Club: Club HQ, Jaguar House, 18 Stuart Street, Luton LU1 2SL. Website: www.jaguardriver.co.uk

Jaguar E-Type Club: PO Box 2, Tenbury Wells, Worcestershire WR15 8XX. Website: www.e-typeclub.com

Jaguar Enthusiasts Club: Abbeywood Office Park, Emma Chris Way, Filton, Bristol BS34 7JU. Website: www.jec.org.uk

Jaguar XK Club: PO Box 2, Tenbury Wells, Worcestershire WR15 8XX. Website: www.xkclub.com

PLACES TO VISIT

Museum displays may be altered and readers are advised to check before travelling that the relevant vehicles are on show, and to ascertain the opening times. An up-to-date listing of all road transport museums in the United Kingdom can be found on www.motormuseums.com.

Coventry Transport Museum, Millennium Place, Hales Street, Coventry CV1 1JD. Telephone: 024 7623 4270. Website: www.transport-museum.com

Haynes International Motor Museum, Sparkford, Yeovil, Somerset BA22 7LH. Telephone: 01963 440804. Website: www.haynesmotormuseum.co.uk

Heritage Motor Centre, Banbury Road, Gaydon, Warwickshire CV35 0BJ. Telephone: 01926 641188. Website: www.heritage-motor-centre.co.uk

National Motor Museum, John Montagu Building, Beaulieu, Brockenhurst, Hampshire SO42 7ZN. Telephone: 01590 612345. Website: www.beaulieu.co.uk